A REBEL'S ROAD

A Rebel's Guide to Recovery

Zachary B. Gorman

Dedication

This book is for the rebels, the misfits, and the seekers of
uncharted paths. To those who've ever felt out of place in the
neatly outlined steps of recovery, "A Rebel's Road" is your
anthem.

It's dedicated to the brave souls who dare to navigate recovery
with a laugh, to those who find strength in their unique journey
towards sobriety. Here's to the ones who choose to write their own
stories, finding light in the darkest of places.

We remember the spirits we've lost to addiction, whose memories
fuel our fight and inspire our steps forward. Their laughter, love,
and lessons remain a beacon of hope and a reminder that we're
not alone in this journey.

To my fellow travelers, may this book offer a companion in your
moments of doubt and a reminder that your path, no matter
how winding, is valid and beautiful. Here's to forging ahead,
embracing your individuality, and discovering that recovery, like
life, is a deeply personal adventure.

-Zachary

CONTENTS

INTRODUCTION

Welcome, fellow misfits, mavericks, and rebels at heart. If you've picked up this guide, chances are you're not looking for the same old sobriety spiel. You're here for something different, something that speaks to the renegade spirit that's gotten you through life's ups and downs thus far. This is "A Rebel's Road: A Rebel's Guide to Recovery," and it's anything but your average recovery book.

Let's get one thing straight: this isn't about preaching or pretending we've got all the answers wrapped up in a neat little package. No, this is about the messy, the gritty, the raw journey of recovery, seen through the eyes of someone who's always taken the road less traveled. It's for those who question, who challenge, and who dare to face their demons with a smirk, saying, "Is that all you've got?"

You see, recovery isn't a one-size-fits-all path. It's a personal journey, as unique as your fingerprint, and it's about damn time we celebrated that. Here, we're tossing out the rulebook and writing our own. We're diving into the heart of addiction, not with fear and trembling, but with courage, humor, and maybe a little bit of that rebel yell.

We'll explore the realities of addiction—not just the darkness and despair, but the moments of absurdity and laughter too. Because if there's one thing true rebels know, it's that humor is our greatest weapon against the seriousness of life. And yes, recovery is serious business, but who says we can't have a few laughs along the way?

This guide will arm you with the tools, stories, and unconventional wisdom needed to navigate your recovery. From the first steps of acknowledging your addiction, through the trials of detox and relapse, to the triumphs of finding your sober tribe and rediscovering joy in a life without substances. And because we know the rebel heart thrives on connection, we'll share stories from fellow travelers on this road, proving that even in our solitude, we're not alone.

But make no mistake, "A Rebel's Road" doesn't sugarcoat the journey. It's not all sunshine and sober rainbows. There will be storms, setbacks, and maybe even a few monsters under the bed. Yet, it's in facing these challenges head-on, with a defiant grin, that we find our true strength.

So, buckle up, dear rebel. You're about to embark on the most important adventure of your life. It's going to be wild, it's going to be weird, but most of all, it's going to be wonderfully, authentically you. Welcome to "A Rebel's Road." Let the journey begin.

CHAPTER 1: "HELLO, IT'S ADDICTION": INTRODUCING THE BEAST

Hey there! Yes, you, picking up this book, probably wondering if these pages hold the magic formula to dance away from addiction like it's some kind of awkwardly persistent salesperson at your doorstep. Well, you're in for a treat – or at least a few chuckles and some hard truths served with a side of empathy.Let's get this out of the way: Addiction isn't a choice, but it's often as misunderstood as a teenager's mood swings. It sneaks up on you, dressed in sheep's clothing, and before you know it, you're wondering how you ended up riding shotgun with a wolf.

What Is Addiction, Really?

Addiction, my soon-to-be-enlightened reader, is like that friend who overstays their welcome at your party. Initially, you're all about the good times, the escape, the laughs. But then, they start raiding your fridge, using your toothbrush, and changing your Netflix password.Scientifically speaking (and yes, we will get a tad serious here), addiction is a complex psychological and physiological process where certain substances or behaviors become so integral to your daily routine that they hijack your brain's reward system. It's like your brain's GPS constantly rerouting you back to the source of addiction, even when you're screaming, "No, I want to go to Sobrietyville!

"The Many Faces of Addiction"

Addiction doesn't always look the same. For some, it's a bottle of booze, for others, a puff, a pill, or even scrolling endlessly through social media (yes, looking at you, Instagram addicts). It could even be something as seemingly benign as running. Ever heard of a runner's high? Well, that's not just the joy of not being chased.Let's not forget the emotional rollercoasters – the gambling, the shopping, the constant need for approval. These are addictions too, my friend. They may not leave a visible mark, but they do a pretty good number on your inner peace.

"But Why Me?"

Ah, the million-dollar question! Why you? Why anyone? Some say it's genetics, like inheriting your grandma's knack for knitting, only less cozy and more destructive. Others argue it's the environment – growing up in a certain way, hanging out with certain crowds. And then there are those who say it's a bit of both, like a disastrous recipe combining family history with a dash of life's chaos.But here's the kicker: Knowing why can be helpful, but it's not the complete roadmap to recovery. That's a journey we're going to explore together, with you in the driver's seat (and me, your humble guide, throwing snacks at you from the back seat).

A Sneak Peek Into Our Journey

This book isn't a lecture series by Dr. Know-It-All. It's more like a road trip with friends who've seen some things, done some stuff, and got the T-shirt to prove it. We'll explore various pathways – from those well-trodden 12 steps to the roads less traveled like meditation, yoga, and maybe some unexpected detours like art therapy or a digital detox.We'll share stories – some of them might be mine, some of them might be yours. We'll laugh (hopefully a lot), we might cry (just a bit), and most importantly, we'll understand that while the journey to recovery isn't a cakewalk, it's definitely a path worth taking.

So, Buckle Up!

You're about to embark on a ride that's part self-discovery, part therapy, and a whole lot of real talk. Addiction might be the uninvited guest in your life, but it's time to show it the door. And don't worry, I'll be right here, guiding you through each step, trick, and flip of the page.So, are you ready? Let's turn this page and step into a world where addiction doesn't call the shots. You do.

CHAPTER 2: "WHY ME?": UNDERSTANDING PERSONAL ADDICTION

Welcome to Chapter 2, where we don our detective hats and turn the magnifying glass inward. Don't worry, this isn't about self-blame or wallowing in self-pity. It's more like becoming a bit of a Sherlock Holmes of your soul. The game is afoot, or rather, the recovery is afoot!

The Mirror Has Two Faces

First things first, let's talk about looking in the mirror. Not just to admire that fabulous face of yours, but to really look. Ask yourself, "What do I see?" Is it someone who's a bit lost, someone who's been partying a tad too hard, or maybe someone who's just been trying to escape life's punches?

The Tale of Two Truths

Here's where we get into the nitty-gritty. There are two truths in the world of addiction: the truth you tell the world and the truth you tell yourself. Sometimes, they're as different as cats and dogs. The world might see a happy, functioning individual, but inside, you might be fighting a battle worthy of an epic saga.

The Checklist Of Realization

- **Let's do a quick checklist. It's like a Buzzfeed quiz, but more** about your life and less about which type of bread you are.

- Do you find yourself thinking about your next drink, puff, bet, or scroll more often than not?
- Are your routines built around your addiction?
- Has someone expressed concern about your habits?
- Do you get defensive or secretive about your addictive behavior?
- Are there times you can't remember what happened while under the influence?
- Do you keep using or doing it, even though you know it's causing problems?
- If you're nodding along to these, it might be time to consider that your guest (addiction) has overstayed its welcome.

The Myth of Rock Bottom

You might have heard that you need to hit rock bottom to start climbing back up. Well, I'm here to tell you that's as true as the tooth fairy managing your dental appointments. You don't have to wait for a cataclysmic event. Your 'rock bottom' can simply be the moment you decide you want a different life.

Acceptance: The First Step on the Yellow Brick Road

Acceptance doesn't mean you're happy about your addiction. It just means you're acknowledging it's there, like a bad tattoo from your teenage years. It's saying, "Yes, this is a part of my life, but it doesn't define me, and I can change it.

"Your Personal 'Why'

Understanding your 'why' can be a game-changer. Why did you start? Why do you continue? And most importantly, why do you want to stop? Your 'why' is your personal beacon, guiding you through the foggy nights on this journey.

A Little Homework (Don't Worry, It's Fun)

Here's a small task for you: Grab a journal or even just a napkin, and write down what you want your life to look like without addiction. Dream big, my friend. This is your canvas, and you're the artist.

Wrapping It Up

You've just taken a huge step simply by reading this chapter and being honest with yourself. Give yourself a pat on the back, or better yet, a high five. You deserve it. In the next chapter, we'll start exploring the tools and strategies for change. But for now, remember this: You're not alone in this, and recognizing your situation is a giant leap forward. It's the first step on a path that's about to get a whole lot brighter.

CHAPTER 3: "THE GREAT ESCAPE": FIRST STEPS AWAY FROM ADDICTION

Alright, brave voyager of self-discovery, you've looked in the mirror, you've nodded (perhaps reluctantly) to a few hard truths. Now, it's time to lace up those metaphorical sneakers because we're about to embark on 'The Great Escape' from the clutches of addiction.

Recognizing the Escape Routes

Every great escape starts with knowing your exit routes. In our case, these aren't fire exits but pathways to a better life. Whether it's through therapy, support groups, or holistic practices, your escape route should feel right for you. This chapter isn't about dictating a one-size-fits-all path but rather about showing you the buffet of options.

Therapy: Not Just for Movie Characters

Therapy can sound daunting, like something out of a dramatic film where someone lies on a couch and talks about their childhood. But it's actually a powerful tool. Whether it's talking to a counselor, diving into cognitive behavioral therapy, or exploring new-age therapies, these sessions can be your private lab for self-exploration and repair.

The Power of Group Therapy and Support Networks

Remember, Frodo didn't go to Mordor alone; he had the Fellowship. Similarly, support groups can be your fellowship. There's power in sharing your journey with others who understand what you're going through. Whether it's a traditional 12-step program or a modern support network, find your tribe.

Holistic Approaches: More Than Just Incense and Yoga Mats

Holistic practices like yoga, meditation, and mindfulness are like giving your brain a spa day. They help in calming the mind, improving focus, and building resilience. And the best part? You can do them in your pajamas!

Getting Physical: Sweat the Addiction Out

Physical activity is a natural antidepressant and a fantastic way to combat addiction. Whether it's joining a local sports team, going for a run, or just doing a funky dance in your living room, get that body moving!

Nutrition: Fueling Your Body and Mind

Your diet can play a huge role in how you feel and, consequently, in your recovery process. Think of food as your body's mechanic, fixing up all the bits and pieces that need a little TLC.

The First Step: Committing to Change

The first step might be small, but it's the most important. It's about making a commitment to yourself. Write it down, say it out loud, tattoo it on your heart (figuratively, of course) - whatever makes it feel real.

Setting Small, Achievable Goals

Think of recovery like building a LEGO castle. You don't start with the whole castle; you start with one brick. Set small, achievable goals – like attending a support group meeting, trying a therapy session, or even just waking up and deciding not to engage in your addictive behavior for that day.

Embracing the Journey Ahead

As we wrap up this chapter, remember that your journey is unique. It might be messy, beautiful, challenging, and exhilarating, often all at once. Embrace it. Every step, every stumble, every leap is part of your story, and it's worth telling.

CHAPTER 4: "THE TOOLBOX": PRACTICAL METHODS FOR EARLY RECOVERY

Welcome to the chapter where we start filling up your toolbox with practical methods for early recovery. Think of this as your personal hardware store, where every tool represents a strategy to help rebuild the house of your life. And don't worry, we'll sprinkle in real stories, including your own and those of your rehab roommates, to see these tools in action.

Understanding Your Tools: A Brief Overview

Before we dive into the stories, let's introduce the tools. These range from journaling and mindfulness to structured routines and creative outlets. Each has its place in your toolbox, ready to be used when the right job (or challenge) comes along.

Journaling: Writing Your Way Through Recovery

Let's start with journaling – it's like having a conversation with yourself on paper. Writing down your thoughts, feelings, and daily experiences can provide clarity and release. Your story, for instance, could begin with your first day in rehab, the mixed emotions, the fears, and the small victories.

Mindfulness: Staying in the Now

Mindfulness is about being fully present in the moment. It's not about silencing your thoughts; it's about observing them without judgment. Remember how you described those early mornings in rehab, watching the sunrise, feeling a mix of anxiety and hope? That's mindfulness – observing your feelings without getting lost in them.

Structured Routines: The Skeleton of Your Day

Establishing a routine can bring a sense of order and purpose. It doesn't have to be military-style; even simple things like regular meal times, exercise, and sleep can form the backbone of your day. Think back to the structured schedule in rehab and how it gradually brought a sense of normalcy and stability.

Exercise: The Physical Anchor

Exercise is a powerhouse tool. It's not just about fitness; it's about releasing endorphins, those feel-good hormones. Remember the story of your roommate, who started with just 10 minutes of walking a day and how it grew into a passion for running? That's the power of physical activity in recovery.

Creative Outlets: Expressing the Unspoken

Creativity can be a refuge. Painting, music, writing, or any form of creative expression can be a way to process emotions that are hard to verbalize. There was that one roommate who found solace in painting, turning chaotic thoughts into beautiful canvases.

Social Connections: Building a Supportive Network

Recovery can be lonely, but you don't have to do it alone.

Reaching out to supportive friends, joining support groups, or even just attending social events can build a network that holds you up. Remember how you formed a bond with your roommates, sharing stories and supporting each other through tough days?

Celebrating Small Wins: Every Step Counts

In recovery, every small step is a victory. Celebrate your daily achievements – be it resisting a craving, attending a therapy session, or just getting out of bed on a tough day. Your story of celebrating 30 days sober with a small cake in rehab is a perfect example of acknowledging and celebrating progress.

Embracing Setbacks as Learning Opportunities

Setbacks aren't failures; they're part of the journey. Each time you stumble, you learn something new about yourself and your recovery. Think of your roommate who relapsed but then came back stronger, with a deeper understanding of his triggers and a renewed commitment to recovery.

Wrapping Up the Chapter

As we close this chapter, remember that your toolbox is unique to you. What works for one person might not work for another, and that's okay. Recovery is not a one-size-fits-all process. It's about finding and using the tools that resonate with you, your story, and your journey.

CHAPTER 5: "MIND GYMNASTICS": INTRODUCTION TO CBT AND MINDFULNESS

Now that your toolbox is starting to fill, Chapter 5 is all about diving deeper into two powerful techniques: Cognitive Behavioral Therapy (CBT) and Mindfulness. Think of them as mind gymnastics; they flex and strengthen your mental muscles, helping you navigate the complex gymnastic routine that is life and recovery.

Cognitive Behavioral Therapy: Rewiring Your Brain

CBT is like having a personal trainer for your brain. It's about identifying those sneaky, negative thought patterns that lead to addictive behaviors and then, systematically, challenging and changing them.

The Basics of CBT

- **Identifying Negative Thoughts:** These are often automatic and rooted in deep-seated beliefs. Recognizing them is the first step. Remember how you initially believed you couldn't cope with stress without your addiction? That was a negative thought pattern.
- **Challenging These Thoughts:** Once identified, you challenge these thoughts. It's like cross-examining a witness in your

mental courtroom. Are these thoughts factual, or are they just opinions based on fear or habit?
- **Replacing with Positive Thoughts:** The final step is to replace these negative thoughts with positive, realistic ones. Instead of thinking, "I can't handle this," you learn to tell yourself, "I can handle this with the right strategies."

Mindfulness: Living in the Present

Mindfulness is about being fully present in the moment, without judgment. It's not about emptying your mind; it's about being aware of your thoughts and feelings without getting swept away by them.

Practicing Mindfulness

Observation: Start by observing your surroundings, your thoughts, your feelings. Like when you first felt the urge to use in rehab, you simply observed the craving without acting on it.

Acceptance: Accept your thoughts and feelings without judgment.Acknowledge them and let them be. It's okay to have cravings or feel anxious; it's part of being human.Living in the Moment: Focus on the here and now. Engage fully with your current activity. Remember the mindfulness exercise where you focused solely on the sensations of eating an orange? The texture, the taste, the smell – all of it.

Real-Life Application of CBT and Mindfulness

Combining CBT and mindfulness can be incredibly effective in recovery. For instance, when you face a trigger, CBT helps you challenge the automatic negative thought that you need to use, while mindfulness allows you to stay grounded and present, observing the craving without succumbing to it.

Stories from Rehab: CBT and Mindfulness

Let's bring in some stories from rehab to see how CBT and mindfulness play out in real life.

Story 1: The Midnight Craving

Remember Jack from rehab? Jack was a night owl, and his toughest cravings hit at midnight. Using CBT, he identified his negative thought: "I can't sleep without using." He challenged it by asking himself if this was indeed true or just a belief. Then, he replaced it with a positive thought: "I can train my body to sleep naturally." He also practiced mindfulness, observing his craving without judgment, focusing on his breathing, and staying present until the craving passed. Over time, his midnight urges weakened.

Story 2: The Social Anxiety Spiral

Maria, another roommate, faced intense social anxiety. Her negative thought pattern was, "I can't be around people without being high." Through CBT, she learned to challenge this belief, questioning its validity. She then replaced it with, "I can learn to be comfortable around people sober." Mindfulness helped Maria stay grounded in social situations, focusing on her breath and the present conversation, not letting anxiety about the future or the past overwhelm her.

Incorporating CBT and Mindfulness into Daily Life

Daily Exercises

- **CBT Journaling:** Start a journal. When you face a negative thought, write it down, challenge it, and then write a more positive, realistic thought.
- **Mindfulness Meditation:** Dedicate a few minutes each day to

mindfulness meditation. Focus on your breath, observe your thoughts and feelings without judgment.
- **Mindful Activities:** Practice being fully present in everyday activities – eating, walking, listening to music. Engage all your senses.

The Bigger Picture

CBT and mindfulness are not just tools for addiction recovery; they are life skills. They improve your relationship with yourself and others and enhance your ability to handle stress and unexpected challenges.

Embracing the Journey

As we close this chapter, remember that mastering CBT and mindfulness takes time and practice. Be patient with yourself. Every day you practice, you're rewiring your brain and strengthening your mental resilience. You're not just recovering from addiction; you're building a stronger, more mindful version of yourself.

CHAPTER 6: "BEND IT LIKE BUDDHA": YOGA AND MEDITATION FOR RECOVERY

Welcome to Chapter 6, where we explore how yoga and meditation can become vital tools in your recovery toolkit. These ancient practices aren't just for the ultra-spiritual or flexible; they're for anyone looking to find a sense of calm, strength, and clarity in their life - qualities essential for overcoming addiction.

Yoga: More Than Just Twisting Yourself into a Pretzel

Yoga is like a Swiss Army knife for wellness; it has a tool for everything - physical health, mental clarity, emotional resilience, and spiritual connection.

The Basics of Yoga

- **Physical Postures (Asanas):** These improve strength, flexibility, and balance. But it's not about nailing a perfect pose; it's about connecting with your body. Remember how, in rehab, simple stretches in the morning helped ease your body's aches and calm your mind?
- **Breathing Techniques (Pranayama):** Breath is life. Controlled breathing in yoga can help manage stress, reduce cravings, and anchor you in the present moment.
- **Meditation and Mindfulness:** Yoga often ends with meditation, a practice that complements mindfulness. It helps in developing an inner observatory, a place of calm

amidst the storm of cravings and emotions.

Meditation: The Art of Inner Stillness

Meditation isn't about turning off your thoughts; it's about learning to observe them without getting entangled. It's like sitting by a river, watching your thoughts float by like leaves on the water's surface.

Meditation in Practice

- **Start Small:** Even five minutes a day can make a difference. Gradually increase the time as you get more comfortable.
- **Focus on Your Breath:** When your mind wanders (and it will), gently bring your attention back to your breath.
- **Use Guided Meditations:** If you find it hard to meditate alone, start with guided meditations. There are plenty of apps and online resources available.

Stories from Rehab: Yoga and Meditation in Action

Story 1: The Skeptic Turns Yogi

Think about Brian from rehab. He started as a skeptic, joking about how yoga was just "fancy stretching." But as he participated more, he noticed changes. His sleep improved, his anxiety decreased, and he found a new way to cope with cravings. Yoga became his go-to tool for maintaining balance.

Story 2: Finding Peace In Silence

Sarah's story is about discovering meditation. Initially restless, sitting still was a challenge for her. But with practice, she found peace in those moments of stillness. Meditation became her refuge, especially on days when her thoughts seemed overwhelming.

Incorporating Yoga and Meditation into Your Recovery

Look for local yoga classes or use online videos to start practicing at home.

- **Consistency is Key:** Try to incorporate a few minutes of yoga and meditation into your daily routine. Consistency will amplify the benefits.
- **Be Patient and Kind to Yourself:** Remember, it's not about perfection. Be patient with your progress and kind to your body and mind.

The Bigger Picture

Yoga and meditation offer more than just physical benefits; they provide a way to reconnect with yourself, to find balance and peace amidst life's turbulence. They teach you to approach your recovery (and life) with mindfulness, compassion, and patience.

Embracing the Journey

As we wrap up this chapter, think of yoga and meditation as your companions on the road to recovery. They are there to help you find strength in vulnerability, calm in chaos, and clarity in confusion. With each pose, each breath, you're not just healing from addiction; you're embarking on a transformative journey towards a more centered and balanced self.

CHAPTER 7: "EAT, SLEEP, REPEAT": THE ROLE OF BASIC HEALTH IN RECOVERY

Welcome to Chapter 7! Here, we dive into the fundamental yet often overlooked pillars of recovery: nutrition, sleep, and routine. These elements are the bedrock of good health, vital for anyone, but especially for someone journeying through recovery.

Nutrition: Feeding the Body and Soul

When battling addiction, it's easy to forget the simple act of eating well. But nutrition plays a crucial role in recovery. It's about more than just filling your stomach; it's about nourishing your body and mind.

The Basics of Nutrition in Recovery

- **Balanced Diet:** Focus on a balanced diet rich in fruits, vegetables, lean proteins, whole grains, and healthy fats. These foods replenish nutrients that may have been depleted by substance abuse.
- **Hydration:** Keep yourself well-hydrated. Water is key to detoxifying and helping your body function optimally.
- **Regular Meal Times:** Establishing regular meal times helps regulate your body's clock, contributing to better physical and mental health.

Sleep: The Unsung Hero of Recovery

Good sleep is like hitting the reset button for your brain. It's when your body repairs itself, and your brain processes the events of the day.

Improving Sleep Quality

- **Create a Sleep-Inducing Environment:** Make your bedroom a sanctuary for sleep – quiet, dark, and cool.
- **Establish a Regular Sleep Schedule:** Go to bed and wake up at the same time every day, even on weekends.
- **Develop a Pre-Sleep Routine:** Engage in calming activities before bed, like reading or listening to soft music.

Routine: The Rhythm of Recovery

Having a routine provides structure, a sense of normalcy, and control – something often lost in the chaos of addiction.

Building Your Routine

- **Start with Small, Manageable Tasks:** Don't overload yourself. Start with small tasks and gradually build your routine.Ensure your routine includes activities that nurture your wellbeing, like exercise, hobbies, or relaxation time.
- **Stay Flexible:** Be willing to adjust your routine as needed. It's a tool to help you, not a strict regime to imprison you.

Stories from Rehab: Nutrition, Sleep, and Routine in Action

Story 1: The Culinary Comeback

Remember Alex from rehab? His journey with nutrition started with learning to cook simple meals. He found that cooking was not just about eating; it was therapeutic. Gradually, as he ate better, he felt better – both physically and emotionally.

Story 2: The Night Owl Finds Her Rhythm

Jenny struggled with sleep, staying up late and feeling exhausted during the day. In rehab, she developed a nighttime routine – a warm bath, a cup of herbal tea, and a chapter of a good book. Slowly, her sleep improved, and with it, her ability to engage more positively in her recovery.

Embracing the Journey

As you close this chapter, remember that taking care of your basic health needs is not a luxury; it's a necessity. Proper nutrition, quality sleep, and a structured routine are not just parts of recovery; they're foundations for a healthy, balanced life. Each meal, each night's rest, each day's routine is a step towards a stronger, healthier you.

CHAPTER 8: "GETTING PHYSICAL: SWEAT THE ADDICTION OUT"

Welcome to Chapter 8, where we lace up our sneakers and dive into the world of exercise and physical activity as vital tools in your recovery arsenal. Remember, this isn't about becoming a marathon runner overnight; it's about using physical movement to heal and strengthen both your body and mind.

The Power of Physical Activity

Exercise is more than just a way to get fit; it's a potent weapon against addiction. It helps reduce stress, improve mood, boost self-esteem, and even alleviate symptoms of depression and anxiety.

Starting Small

- **Find an Activity You Enjoy:** Whether it's walking, swimming, yoga, or dancing, the best exercise is one you enjoy and will stick with.
- **Set Realistic Goals:** Start with achievable goals. It could be as simple as a 10-minute walk each day. Gradually increase the duration and intensity as you get stronger.
- **Consistency is Key:** Try to be consistent. Regular physical activity, even in small doses, can make a significant difference.

The Link Between Exercise and Mental Health

Physical activity releases endorphins, the body's natural mood lifters. It also helps in reducing cortisol, the stress hormone. This biochemical change is a natural antidote to the lows of addiction withdrawal.

Mental Benefits

- **Improved Mood:** Regular exercise can lead to an enhanced sense of well-being.
- **Stress Relief:** Physical activity is a great way to manage stress, a common trigger for relapse.
- **Better Sleep:** Regular exercise can improve sleep patterns, essential for recovery.

Stories from Rehab: The Transformative Power of Exercise

Story 1: The Runner's High Replaced The Other High

Mike discovered running in rehab. Initially, it was just a way to pass the time, but soon he found it meditative. The physical exertion became a healthy outlet for his frustrations and anxieties, replacing the need for his addiction.

Story 2: Yoga As A Path To Inner Peace

Lisa found solace in yoga. It wasn't just the physical poses that helped; the breathwork and meditative aspects of yoga gave her tools to deal with cravings and anxiety. Her story is a testament to how integrating mind and body practices can be transformative in recovery.

Making Exercise a Part of Your Recovery Plan

- **Join a Class or Group:** Sometimes, being part of a group can be motivating. Look for local sports teams, exercise classes, or walking groups.
- **Exercise Safely:** Listen to your body. If you're new to exercise or have health concerns, consult a professional first.
- **Track Your Progress:** Keep a journal of your physical activity. Celebrating your progress can be incredibly rewarding and motivating.

Embracing the Journey

As this chapter concludes, remember that incorporating physical activity into your recovery is not just about improving your physical health; it's a crucial step in rebuilding your life, restoring your mental balance, and rediscovering joy. Every step, every stretch, every breath is a step towards a stronger, more resilient you

CHAPTER 9: "THE TECHY SIDE OF RECOVERY: NAVIGATING THE DIGITAL JUNGLE WITH A SMILE"

Alright, digital warriors of the modern age, welcome to the jungle – the digital jungle, that is. In Chapter 9, we're swinging through the vines of technology to discover how it can be more than just a black hole of cat videos and memes in your recovery journey. Let's add a pinch of humor and a dash of wisdom as we explore this brave new world.

The Digital Dance: Finding Your Rhythm

Think of technology in recovery like learning a new dance. At first, you're all thumbs and two left feet, but soon you find the rhythm. From sobriety apps that cheer you on like a digital cheerleader to meditation apps that soothe your soul better than a cup of herbal tea, we've got it all here.

Sobriety Trackers: Your Pocket-Sized Cheerleaders

- **Celebrate Every Win:** These apps don't just count days; they throw a mini-party for every milestone you hit. Imagine a little digital confetti explosion for each day you stay sober.
- **Motivation Galore:** Get ready for motivational quotes that are cheesier than a double cheese pizza but surprisingly uplifting.

- **Visualize Your Victory:** There's something deeply satisfying about seeing your progress charted out. It's like leveling up in a video game, but the prize is your well-being.

Zen in Your Pocket: Mindfulness Apps

These apps are like having a monk in your pocket. Whether you're in line at the supermarket or taking a break at work, you can whip out your phone and bam – instant Zen.

Guided Meditations: Like GPS for Your Soul

- **Customizable Calm:** Whether you have 2 minutes or 20, there's a meditation waiting for you. It's like ordering a latte; pick your flavor of peace.
- **A Breath of Fresh Air:** These apps remind you to breathe – something so simple yet so easy to forget, especially when your cravings hit like a tsunami.

Virtual Reality: The Recovery Simulator

Imagine strapping on a VR headset and stepping into a world where you can practice coping strategies in lifelike scenarios. It's like rehearsing for a play, but the play is your life, and the lead role is yours.

Virtual Reality Therapy: A New Frontier

- **Simulated Scenarios:** Face triggers and practice coping skills in a safe, controlled virtual environment. It's like a flight simulator, but for navigating the challenges of sobriety.
- **Emotional Immersion:** VR can evoke realistic emotions and responses, giving you a chance to understand and manage your reactions in a safe space.
- **Online Support Groups:** Your Digital TribeThese are like the local coffee shop of the digital world – places to share stories,

offer support, and feel connected, all while in your pajamas.

Finding Your People

- **Diverse Communities:** Whether you're into knitting or skydiving, there's a group for you. It's like a buffet of support; take what you need.
- **Anonymity with a Heart:** Share your journey without the pressure of revealing your identity. It's like being a superhero with a secret identity, but your power is resilience.

The Cautionary Tale: Don't Let Tech Rule Your Life!

Now, let's not forget that while technology is fantastic, it's a bit like chocolate - great in moderation, but too much, and you're down a rabbit hole watching videos of squirrels water-skiing at 3 AM.

Balancing Act

- **Digital Detox:** Every now and then, unplug yourself. Go outside. Remember trees? Those green things? They're pretty cool.
- **Real People, Real Connections:** Use technology to enhance, not replace, real-world relationships. There's no app that can replicate a hug or a high-five (yet).
- **Mindful Usage:** Be conscious of how you're using technology. Is it serving your recovery, or are you just scrolling through your ex's vacation photos?

Embracing the Journey with a Techy Twist

As we wrap up this tech-savvy chapter, remember that in the digital dance of recovery, you're the DJ. Mix and match the tools that work for you. Use technology as a stepping stone, not a crutch, and keep your journey towards recovery as real and grounded as possible - with the occasional digital sprinkle of magic.

. . . .

CHAPTER 10: "THE ROCKY ROAD: NAVIGATING RELAPSES AND SETBACKS"

Welcome to Chapter 10, where we talk about the bumpy part of the journey – relapses and setbacks. Think of this chapter as your trusty shock absorber for the rocky road of recovery. We're going to navigate these bumps with a mix of humor, honesty, and strategies that are more useful than a Swiss Army knife in a survival show.

Relapse: Not the End, Just a Detour

First off, let's reframe how we view relapse. It's not the end of the world, although it might feel like it. It's more like taking a wrong turn on your road trip. Sure, it's frustrating, but it's also a chance to recalibrate your GPS and get back on track.

Understanding Relapse

- **It's Part of the Process:** Many people in recovery experience relapses. It doesn't mean failure; it means you're human and recovery is challenging.
- **Learning Opportunity:** Each relapse is a learning opportunity. What triggered it? How did you respond? It's like being a detective in your own life, minus the cool hat.

Strategies to Navigate Setbacks

So, how do we deal with these setbacks? With tools, tactics, and a bit of tenacity, that's how!

Prevention First

- **Know Your Triggers:** Like a superhero understanding their weaknesses, know what situations, emotions, or people might trigger a relapse.
- **Have a Plan:** Develop a relapse prevention plan. Think of it as your emergency kit – something you hope not to use, but it's there, just in case.

In The Moment

- **Mindfulness:** Stay present. Acknowledge what you're feeling. It's about recognizing the wave of craving and choosing not to surf it.
- **Reach Out:** Call your support person, therapist, or a trusted friend. Sometimes, just voicing your feelings can take the power out of them.

Embracing the Bumps

Remember, the road to recovery isn't a straight highway; it's more like a scenic route with twists and turns. Each bump, each detour, adds to your story and builds your resilience.

Resilience Building

- **Self-Compassion:** Be kind to yourself. Talk to yourself like you would to a dear friend who's struggling.
- **Reflect and Learn:** After a setback, take time to reflect. What can you learn from it? How can you strengthen your strategies?

Your Comeback Story

Every time you bounce back from a setback, you're writing your comeback story. And let me tell you, those are the best kinds of stories. They have drama, suspense, and a hero who overcomes the odds – that's you, by the way.

Wrapping Up

As we close Chapter 10, remember that the path of recovery is a bit like a dance – sometimes you step forward, sometimes you step back, and occasionally, you step on your own toes. But the important thing is to keep dancing, keep moving forward. Relapses and setbacks are not signs of defeat; they're just part of the dance, part of your journey to a stronger and wiser you.

CHAPTER 11: "EMBRACING CHANGE: BEHAVIORAL AND LIFESTYLE ADJUSTMENTS"

Buckle up, dear readers! Chapter 11 is like the wardrobe to Narnia, but instead of talking lions and witches, we're exploring the magical world of change. Here, we'll learn how to embrace both the monumental and the minuscule changes in our journey to recovery – with a few laughs along the way, of course.

The Butterfly Effect in Recovery

Change in recovery can be like the butterfly effect. You make one small change, and before you know it, it's set off a tornado of positive transformations in your life. Who knew that deciding to take a morning walk could eventually lead to you running a half-marathon?

Small Steps, Big Impact

- **Routine Tweaks:** Start with something small. Swap out one habit for a healthier one. It's like choosing a salad over fries – initially less exciting, but your heart (and body) will thank you later.
- **Mindful Mornings:** How you start your day can set the tone for the rest. Instead of rolling out of bed and into chaos, try a morning ritual – meditation, stretching, writing, or just enjoying a quiet cup of tea.

Laughing in the Face of Change

Let's be honest, change can be as scary as watching a horror movie alone at night. But it can also be exciting. It's all about perspective. And a good laugh can make anything less intimidating

Finding Humor In The Process

- **Embrace the Absurd:** Ever tried laughing at your mistakes instead of beating yourself up?
- **Celebrate the Quirky:** Each small change you make might feel odd at first, like wearing socks with sandals. But hey, if it works for you, embrace the quirkiness

The Domino Effect of Lifestyle Choices

Every good choice you make tends to knock over another domino, leading to more positive choices. It's like upgrading from a flip phone to a smartphone - suddenly, you realize there's so much more you can do.

Harnessing Positive Momentum

- **Healthy Eating:** Good nutrition isn't just about losing weight; it's about feeling better mentally and physically. It's like fueling your car with premium gas instead of that questionable discount stuff.
- **Active Living:** Incorporating more activity into your day doesn't mean you have to become a gym rat. Dance while doing the dishes, walk to the store, or have animated talks with your hands – every bit counts!

Embracing the New You

With each change, you're not just moving away from addiction; you're moving towards a new version of yourself.

Think of it as an upgrade – Recovery 2.0.

Identity Beyond Addiction

- **Rediscover Interests:** Remember that hobby you had before addiction took center stage? It's time to rekindle old flames – whether it's painting, playing the guitar, or collecting stamps.New

- **Social Circles:** As you change, so might your social circles. It's like diversifying your portfolio – different friends for different aspects of your new life

Navigating Resistance to Change

It's natural to face some resistance, both from within and from others. Change can be uncomfortable, like wearing a new pair of shoes. But eventually, they mold to your feet

Dealing With Internal Resistance

- **Self-Talk:** When you hear that little voice saying, "This is too hard," respond with, "But not impossible." Be your own cheerleader.
- **Patience is Key:** Remember, Rome wasn't built in a day, and neither is the new you. Give yourself the grace to grow at your own pace

Wrapping Up

As we tie up Chapter 11, keep in mind that embracing change is about enjoying the journey as much as the destination. It's about finding joy in the new paths you carve and the new person you become along the way. Sure, there will be days when change feels as comfortable as a sweater in a heatwave, but remember, every step forward, no matter how small, is a victory in itself.

CHAPTER 12: "YOUR STORY, YOUR SUPERPOWER: SHARING YOUR JOURNEY"

Brace yourselves, storytellers and listeners alike, as we dive into Chapter 12! Here, we're about to embark on an epic quest – the quest of storytelling in recovery. It's like becoming the author of your own adventure novel, where the hero (spoiler alert: it's you) overcomes challenges and discovers their superpower: their story.

The Magic of Storytelling

Think of your recovery journey as a treasure trove of experiences, lessons, and insights. Sharing your story isn't just about narrating events; it's about transforming your experiences into a beacon of hope and understanding, both for yourself and others.

Why Your Story Matters

- **Connection:** Sharing creates connections, breaking down the walls of isolation that addiction often builds.
- **Empowerment:** Every time you share your story, you take ownership of your journey. It's like saying, "This is my story, and I'm the one writing the chapters."

Crafting Your Narrative

Your story is unique, and how you tell it can make all the difference. Whether it's through writing, speaking, art, or music, find the medium that resonates with you.

Tips For Sharing

- **Be Authentic:** Your story is powerful because it's real. Embrace the good, the bad, and the ugly – it's all part of the beautiful tapestry of your life.
- **Respect Your Comfort Zone:** Share what you're comfortable sharing. It's not about airing all your laundry – just the pieces you're okay with showing.

The Healing Power of Storytelling

Storytelling isn't just about inspiring others; it's a therapeutic tool for the storyteller. It allows you to process your experiences, reflect on your journey, and make sense of your past.

Reflection Through Narration

- **Understanding Patterns:** As you share your story, you might start to see patterns in your behavior or thinking that weren't obvious before.
- **Emotional Release:** Speaking your truth can be incredibly liberating. It's like releasing a balloon you've been holding down – up, up, and away goes the weight of those emotions.

Ripple Effect

Every time you share your story, you create ripples. You never know whose life you might touch, whose path you might illuminate, or who might see a reflection of themselves in your narrative.

Inspiring Others

- **Hope and Courage**: For someone just starting their recovery journey, your story can be a lighthouse in a stormy sea – a beacon of hope and a testament to the courage it takes to change.

- **Building a Community:** Your story can help forge a community of understanding and support. It's like inviting others to sit around your campfire, sharing warmth and light in the darkness.

Navigating the Challenges of Storytelling

Not every storytelling experience will be a walk in the park. Sometimes, it can feel like you're a comedian performing to a room full of crickets. But that's okay.

Handling Vulnerability

- **Embrace Vulnerability:** Sharing your story can make you feel exposed, but remember, vulnerability is a strength, not a weakness. It's the courage to show up and be seen.
- **Dealing with Reactions:** Not everyone will respond to your story the way you expect. Prepare yourself for a range of reactions, and remember, their responses are more about them than you.

Your Story's Impact

You might not realize it, but your story can have a profound impact, not just on others, but on you as well. It's like throwing a pebble into a pond – the ripples spread far and wide.

Transforming Lives, Including Yours

- **A Source of Strength:** Each time you share your journey, you reinforce your own strength and commitment to recovery.
- **A Legacy of Hope:** Your story becomes a legacy, a hopeful message to future generations that recovery is possible, and

change can happen.

Wrapping Up

As we conclude Chapter 12, remember that your story is a superpower. It has the ability to heal, connect, inspire, and transform. Whether you whisper it to a close friend or shout it from the rooftops, your journey can be a guiding light for someone lost in the dark and a reminder of how far you've come.

CHAPTER 13: "JEDI MIND TRICKS: ADVANCED MINDFULNESS AND COPING STRATEGIES"

Welcome to Chapter 13, where we turn into mental ninjas, mastering the art of advanced mindfulness and coping strategies. Imagine channeling your inner Yoda, finding peace in the midst of chaos, and using your mind like a lightsaber to cut through the darkness of addiction. Let's embark on this epic mental adventure with a dose of humor and a splash of wisdom.

The Next Level of Mindfulness

You've heard about mindfulness, but now it's time to take it up a notch. We're not just sitting quietly and breathing; we're becoming mindfulness warriors, using these skills in the thick of life's battles.

Mindfulness 2.0

- **Mindful Living:** This is about integrating mindfulness into every moment. Whether you're brushing your teeth, taking a shower, or waiting in line at the store, every moment is an opportunity for mindfulness.
- **Emotional Awareness:** Become an expert in identifying and observing your emotions. It's like being a weatherman for your feelings – "Today, we have a high chance of irritability

with a slight breeze of sadness in the evening."

Coping Strategies for the Modern World

Let's face it, the world can be as unpredictable as a cat on catnip. That's why having a toolbox of coping strategies is essential.

The Coping Toolkit

- **Crisis Survival Techniques:** Learn techniques like deep breathing, grounding, and sensory awareness to help you navigate through acute cravings or emotional storms.
- **Long-Term Coping Skills:** Develop skills like assertive communication, setting healthy boundaries, and time management. These are like your mental gym – the more you practice, the stronger you get.

Harnessing the Power of Visualization

Visualization isn't just for athletes or daydreamers; it's a powerful tool in recovery. It's like building your dream house, but in your mind, and you're the architect.

Visualization Exercises

- **Future Self:** Visualize your future self – the version of you that's overcome addiction. What do they look like? What are they doing? It's a bit like time travel without the pesky paradoxes.
- **Safe Place Visualization:** Create a mental sanctuary – a place you can retreat to when you need peace and calm. It could be a beach, a forest, a cozy room – anywhere that soothes your soul.

The Art of Letting Go

One of the toughest yet most liberating parts of mindfulness is learning the art of letting go – letting go of control, of expectations, of the past.

Practicing Detachment

- **Acceptance:** Learn to accept things as they are, not as you wish them to be. It's like being in a traffic jam and deciding to listen to your favorite podcast instead of honking furiously.
- **Non-attachment:** Practice holding things lightly, whether it's emotions, outcomes, or even relationships. It's about caring deeply, yet not clinging desperately.

Coping Strategies: The Mental Gymnastics

Life throws curveballs, but with the right coping strategies, you're ready to catch them or deftly dodge.

Dynamic Coping Skills

- **Stress Management Techniques:** Learn to manage stress with activities like yoga, tai chi, or even just a walk in the park. It's about finding your zen in the chaos of everyday life.
- **Problem-Solving Skills:** Develop the ability to identify problems and brainstorm solutions, rather than resorting to addictive behaviors. It's like being a detective in your own life – Sherlock Holmes-style.

The 12-Step Integration

The 12-step program offers a wealth of wisdom that can be integrated with mindfulness and coping techniques for a powerful combination.

Combining Principles With Practice

- **Step 1 - Powerlessness and Acceptance:** Recognize and mindfully accept what you can and cannot control. It's the first step towards empowerment.
- **Step 4 - Moral Inventory:** Take a mindful approach to self-reflection. It's not about self-judgment; it's about self-awareness.
- **Steps 8 and 9 - Amends:** Use mindful communication and empathy when making amends, ensuring your actions are thoughtful and genuine.

More Visualization and Affirmations

Harness the power of your mind with visualization techniques and affirmations. It's like building your dream life, one thought at a time.

Techniques For Success

- **Goal Visualization:** Regularly visualize your goals and aspirations. Imagine your success in vivid detail – it's like daydreaming with a purpose.
- **Daily Affirmations:** Reinforce your journey with positive affirmations. Repeat empowering phrases that resonate with your soul, like a personal mantra.

Mindful Relapse Prevention

Relapse prevention is a key component of recovery. Integrating mindfulness into this process can make it more effective and sustainable.

Strategies For Mindful Relapse Prevention

- **Trigger Awareness:** Develop a deep awareness of your triggers. Use mindfulness to observe these triggers without judgment, understanding their power but also your capacity to respond differently.
- **Mindful Response to Cravings:** When cravings arise, instead of reacting impulsively, pause. Observe the craving with detachment, acknowledging its presence but choosing not to act on it.
- **Step 10 - Continued Inventory and Mindfulness:** Regularly practice self-reflection as advised in Step 10 of the 12-Step program, but with a mindful approach. Acknowledge your successes and areas for growth with compassion and without judgment.

Integrating the 12 Steps with Mindfulness

The principles of the 12-Step program can beautifully complement your mindfulness practice, creating a holistic approach to recovery.

Harmonizing The Two Approaches

- **Steps 2 and 3 - Higher Power and Surrender:** Use mindfulness to explore your understanding of a Higher Power. It's about finding a spiritual connection that resonates with you, in a mindful, introspective manner.
- **Step 11 - Meditation and Prayer:** This step focuses on improving conscious contact with a Higher Power through prayer and meditation. Deepen this practice with mindfulness, enhancing your spiritual connection and self-awareness.

Advanced Techniques for Emotional Regulation

Emotional regulation is crucial in recovery. Advanced

mindfulness techniques can provide you with the skills to manage your emotions effectively.Emotion-Focused Practices

- **Body Scanning for Emotional Awareness:** Regularly practice body scanning to become more aware of how emotions manifest physically in your body.
- **Mindful Journaling:** Keep a journal where you not only record your thoughts and experiences but also practice being present with and processing your emotions mindfully.

Wrapping Up

As we conclude Chapter 13, remember that the path of recovery is as much about mastering your mind as it is about abstaining from substances. The advanced mindfulness techniques and coping strategies, combined with the timeless wisdom of the 12-Step program, create a powerful toolkit for navigating the journey of recovery. You're not just surviving; you're thriving, growing, and evolving into the best version of yourself - a true mental Jedi.

CHAPTER 14: "THE HAPPINESS PROJECT: FINDING JOY IN SOBRIETY"

Welcome to Chapter 14, where we embark on a delightful expedition to unearth the joys hidden in the nooks and crannies of sobriety. Picture this chapter as a treasure map, leading you to the X-marks-the-spot of happiness in your sober life. Let's set sail on this adventure with a compass of optimism and a spyglass of humor!

Reimagining Joy in Sobriety

Sobriety isn't just about removing something from your life; it's about adding so much more. It's like clearing out your attic and discovering it's a great place for a new art studio or a cozy reading nook.

Discovering New Passions

- **Explore New Interests**: Sobriety is the perfect time to try new hobbies or revisit old ones. Ever wanted to learn guitar, bake sourdough bread, or salsa dance? Now's your chance.
- **Connect with Nature:** There's something inherently joyful about being in nature. Whether it's hiking, gardening, or just picnicking in the park, let Mother Nature be your therapist.

The Small Joys: Celebrating Everyday Victories

In the journey of recovery, every day you maintain your

sobriety is a victory. These daily triumphs are the building blocks of a joyous sober life.

Finding Joy In The Ordinary

- **Mindful Appreciation:** Practice mindfulness to savor everyday moments – the aroma of your morning coffee, the feeling of sun on your face, the laughter of a friend.
- **Gratitude Journaling:** Keep a gratitude journal. Writing down even the smallest things you're thankful for can shift your focus from what's missing to what's abundant in your life.

Building a Joyful Community

The people around us play a significant role in our happiness. In sobriety, building a community of supportive and positive individuals is crucial.

Cultivating Positive Relationships

- **Join Supportive Groups:** Whether it's a sobriety support group or a hobby club, connect with people who uplift you.
- **Volunteer Your Time:** Volunteering can be a source of deep joy. Giving back not only helps others but fills you with a sense of purpose and connection.

Embracing the New You

Sobriety offers the opportunity to rediscover who you are without the influence of substances. It's like meeting yourself for the first time – and you might be pleasantly surprised.

Self-Discovery And Growth

- **Personal Development:** Invest time in personal development.

Read books, attend workshops, or simply spend time reflecting on your personal growth.

- **Celebrate Your Sobriety Milestones:** Each milestone in your sobriety journey deserves celebration. Treat yourself to something special – you've earned it!

The Role of Laughter and Play

Never underestimate the power of laughter and play in recovery. They're not just for kids; they're essential ingredients for a happy life.

Incorporating Fun

- **Find Reasons to Laugh:** Watch comedies, share jokes with friends, or just laugh at the absurdities of life.
- **Be Playful:** Engage in playful activities – have a game night, go to a theme park, or play a sport just for fun.

Wrapping Up

As we close Chapter 14, remember that finding joy in sobriety is a journey, not a destination. It's about rediscovering the pleasures in life that addiction may have overshadowed. Embrace this journey with an open heart and a curious spirit, and watch as your life in recovery blooms with unexpected joys and fulfilling experiences.

CHAPTER 15: "GIVING BACK: THE CIRCLE OF SUPPORT IN RECOVERY"

Welcome to Chapter 15, where we embark on a heartwarming journey of giving back. In the world of recovery, the act of helping others isn't just a good deed; it's a vital part of the healing process. Imagine this chapter as a guide to planting seeds of kindness and watching them bloom into a garden of support and community.

The Power of Helping Others

Helping others in their recovery journey can bring a sense of purpose, fulfillment, and connection. It's like lighting a candle from yours – it doesn't diminish your light, but brightens the world a bit more.

Why Giving Back Matters

- **Strengthens Your Own Recovery:** Teaching is the best way to learn. By supporting others, you reinforce your own commitment to sobriety.
- **Builds Community**: Being part of a support network creates a sense of belonging and shared purpose.

Volunteering: A Pathway to Purpose

Volunteering offers a chance to step outside yourself and contribute to something bigger. It's a powerful way to build self-esteem and find purpose in your sobriety.

Opportunities To Volunteer

- **•Recovery Groups and Programs:** Share your experience and strength in recovery groups or mentor someone who is new to recovery.
- **Community Service:** Engage in local community service projects. Whether it's a soup kitchen, a community garden, or a charity event, every bit of help counts.

Mentorship: Guiding the Way for Others

Becoming a mentor to someone in early recovery is both a privilege and a responsibility. It's like being a lighthouse for a ship navigating through foggy waters.

Being A Mentor

- **Sharing Your Story:** Offer insights and lessons from your own journey. Your experiences can be a valuable guide for others.Listening and
- **Supporting:** Sometimes, themost valuable thing you can offer is an empathetic ear. Listening and providing support can make a huge difference in someone's recovery journey.

The Benefits of Peer Support

Engaging in peer support groups isn't just about getting help; it's also about giving it. The mutual exchange of support and understanding is a cornerstone of the recovery community.

Participating In Support Groups

- **Sharing Experiences:** In group settings, sharing your story can inspire and encourage others.

- **Offering Encouragement:** Celebrate the successes of others and offer comfort during challenging times. A few words of encouragement can go a long way.

Learning Through Teaching

In the process of helping others, you often gain new insights into your own journey. Teaching or sharing knowledge can deepen your understanding of recovery principles.

Educational Roles

- **Conduct Workshops or Seminars:** If you have a skill or knowledge area that can benefit others, consider leading a workshop or seminar.Write or Blog: Share your experiences and insights through writing. Starting a blog or contributing to recovery publications can help reach a wider audience.

The Ripple Effect of Kindness

Every act of kindness in the recovery community creates ripples that extend far beyond the immediate interaction. You might not always see the impact, but it's there – growing and spreading.

Impact Beyond Sight

- **Inspirational Influence:** Your actions might inspire others to give back, creating a positive cycle of support and kindness.
- **Building a Stronger Community:** Every individual who is supported becomes a stronger member of the community, enhancing the collective resilience and resources

Wrapping Up

In Chapter 15, we've explored the fulfilling journey of

giving back and how it not only enriches the lives of others but also adds depth and meaning to our own recovery. As we close this chapter, remember that in the ecosystem of recovery, every act of kindness, every word of support, and every gesture of understanding contributes to a stronger, more vibrant community.

CHAPTER 16: "LAUGHING MATTERS: THE SERIOUS BUSINESS OF HAVING FUN IN RECOVERY"

Strap in, dear readers, for Chapter 16 – where we dive into the lighter side of life in recovery. Remember, sobriety doesn't mean a life sentence in the land of boredom. It's quite the opposite; it's your VIP pass to the joyous carnival of life. So, let's rediscover the forgotten art of having fun, with a few chuckles along the way!

Rediscovering Joy and Laughter

In the whirlwind of recovery, we sometimes forget that it's okay – no, essential – to have fun. It's like finally getting off a tedious, never-ending escalator and jumping onto a merry-go-round.

Embracing the Lighter Side of Life

- ●**Find Your Funny:** Whether it's stand-up comedy, funny movies, or dad jokes, find something that tickles your funny bone.
- ●**Laughter Yoga:** Yes, it's a thing! Combining laughter exercises with yoga breathing, it's like a workout for your soul and abs at the same time.

Story Time: The Joy of Recovery

Let's sprinkle in some real-life tales of rediscovering joy in recovery. These stories are like little beams of sunshine on a cloudy day.

Story 1: Mike's Karaoke Comeback

Mike always thought karaoke was just for wannabe pop stars and shower singers. But in recovery, he discovered it was a fantastic way to let loose. His rendition of "I Will Survive" wasn't just a song choice; it was his recovery anthem. The applause he received wasn't for his singing skills (which, let's be honest, were comparable to a cat in a wind tunnel), but for his infectious joy.

Story 2:Sarah's Roller Derby Debut

Sarah found her laughter on roller skates. Joining a roller derby team, she swapped her addiction for adrenaline and camaraderie. Each bout was a mix of fierce competition and comic falls – think of it as bumper cars on roller skates. The bruises were real, but so were the fits of laughter and the sense of belonging.

Fun Activities: The Recovery Playbook

Who says recovery can't be fun? Here's a playbook of activities to inject some excitement into your sober life.

A List Of Joy-Inducing Activities

- **Outdoor Adventures:** Hiking, biking, or even star-gazing. Nature is like a giant playground waiting to be explored. And remember, getting lost is half the fun (as long as you have GPS to find your way back).
- **Creative Endeavors:** Painting, writing, pottery – let your inner artist run wild. It's like giving a toddler finger paints and

saying, "Go nuts!"

- **Group Sports or Activities:** Join a local sports league, a dance class, or a trivia team. It's not about winning (though that's nice), it's about the laughs and high-fives along the way.

The Benefits of Fun in Recovery

Having fun in recovery isn't just a way to pass time; it's a process. It recharges your batteries, boosts your mood, and strengthens your resolve to stay on the path of sobriety.

Why Laughter Really Is The Best Medicine

- **Stress Relief:** Laughter reduces stress hormones and releases endorphins. It's like giving your mind a mini-vacation.
- **Improved Social Connections:** Shared laughter can help forge stronger bonds with friends and family. It's the glue in relationships, minus the sticky mess.
- **Finding Balance:** Fun and ResponsibilityIt's important to balance fun with the responsibilities of daily life.Think of it as juggling – you want to keep all the balls in the air, but it's okay if you drop one now and then. Just pick it back up and keep going.

Striking The Right Chord

- **Scheduled Fun:** Sometimes you need to plan for fun. It sounds counterintuitive, but a little structure ensures you're balancing joy with responsibilities.
- **Mindful Enjoyment:** When you're having fun, be fully present in the moment. Whether it's laughing at a movie or playing a game, immerse yourself in the joy of the activity without letting other concerns intrude.

Embracing New Hobbies and Interests

Sobriety is a chance to rediscover old interests or develop new ones. It's like opening a door to a room you never knew existed in your own house.

Exploring New Horizons

- **Try New Things:** Be bold and try activities you've never considered before. You might find joy in the most unexpected places.
- **Revisit Past Interests:** Reconnect with hobbies that you might have neglected. It's like meeting an old friend and realizing why you got along so well in the first place.

Wrapping Up

As we conclude Chapter 16, remember that fun and laughter are not just add-ons to your recovery journey; they are integral parts of it. They bring lightness to the heart and a spring to the step, making the road of recovery a path of joy and discovery. So go ahead, laugh out loud, dance in the rain, and embrace the joyous side of sobriety!

CHAPTER 17: "SOCIAL BUTTERFLIES: CRAFTING CONNECTIONS IN RECOVERY"

Welcome to Chapter 17! Here, we're going to transform into social butterflies, fluttering into the world of meaningful connections and robust support networks. Think of this chapter as your guide to building a social life that's as colorful and vibrant as a garden in full bloom – all in the world of recovery.

The Importance of Connection

Recovery isn't a solo expedition; it's more like a group hike where everyone supports each other. Building a network of positive relationships is crucial – it's like having a safety net made of friendship and understanding.

Why Relationships Matter

- **Support and Understanding:** Surrounding yourself with people who understand your journey can provide invaluable support on tough days.
- **Shared Experiences:** Connecting with others in recovery allows you to share experiences, advice, and encouragement.

Navigating Social Situations

The social world can be tricky to navigate in sobriety, especially when many social events revolve around substances. It's like playing a game of Twister – you need to find the right balance without toppling over.

Tips For Sober Socializing

- **Sober Gatherings:** Seek out or organize social events that don't revolve around alcohol or substances.
- **The Sober Buddy System:** Bring a friend who understands your journey to social events for support.

Making New Friends, the Adult Way

Making friends as an adult can feel as awkward as a middle school dance, but it's not impossible. It's about finding your tribe – people who share your interests and values.

Finding Your People

- **Hobbies and Interest Groups:** Join clubs or groups that align with your hobbies. Love books? Join a book club. Passionate about hiking? Find a local hiking group.
- **Recovery Groups:** Engaging in recovery groups or sober communities can lead to deep, meaningful friendships.

Rekindling Old Friendships

Sobriety might also mean revisiting old friendships that were overshadowed by addiction. It's like dusting off an old, cherished book and rediscovering its value.

Reaching Out

- **Make the First Move:** Reach out to old friends you might have lost touch with. A simple message can re-open doors.
- **Be Honest:** Share your journey with them. True friends will support and respect your path to recovery.

The Art of Communication

Good communication is key to building and maintaining healthy relationships. It's like being a gardener; you need to nurture your connections for them to grow.

Effective Communication Skills

- **Active Listening:** Be an active listener – it shows you value the other person's thoughts and feelings.
- **Express Yourself Clearly:** Share your thoughts and feelings openly and honestly, but with consideration for the other person's perspective.

Wrapping Up

In Chapter 17, we've explored the art of building and nurturing relationships in recovery. Remember, the connections you make are more than just a support network; they're a reflection of your new sober life.

CHAPTER 18: "REDISCOVERING ME: CRAFTING A NEW IDENTITY IN SOBRIETY"

Welcome to Chapter 18, the chapter where you embark on an exciting journey of self-discovery, akin to an archeological dig where you unearth the amazing treasures of your true self, buried under the sands of addiction. Sobriety isn't just about subtracting a habit; it's about rediscovering and reinventing who you are.

The Blank Canvas of Sobriety

Think of sobriety as a blank canvas. Now,you're the artist with the freedom to paint your new identity. It's like having an all-access pass to the art supplies store of life – every color, every brush, is yours to explore and experiment with.

Embracing The New You

- **Explore Your Interests:** Delve into hobbies and activities to discover what truly excites and fulfills you. It's like trying different flavors at an ice cream shop until you find your favorite.
- **Values and Beliefs:** Sobriety is a chance to reassess what really matters to you. It's like recalibrating your internal compass to guide you toward your true north.

The Adventure of Self-Exploration

Rediscovering yourself can be an adventure, filled with surprises and insights. It's about peeling back the layers to reveal the essence of who you are.

- **Steps in Self-Discovery Journaling:** Write down your thoughts and feelings. It's like having a conversation with yourself on paper.
- **Personality Tests and Quizzes:** These can be fun and enlightening tools in understanding different facets of your personality.

Building Confidence in Your New Identity

As you explore your new identity, building confidence is key. It's like learning to ride a bike – wobbly at first, but exhilarating once you find your balance.

Confidence-Building Strategies

- **Celebrate Small Wins:** Acknowledge and celebrate your achievements, no matter how small. Each one is a stepping stone to greater confidence.
- **Positive Affirmations:** Use positive affirmations to reinforce your self-worth and belief in your new identity.

Navigating Social Dynamics

With a new identity comes new dynamics in social relationships. It's like updating your operating system – you need to figure out how the new version interacts with the world.

Adapting To Change

- **Open Communication:** Be open about your journey with friends and family. It helps set the stage for healthier interactions.

- **Setting Boundaries:** Learn to set boundaries that protect your sobriety and respect your new identity.

Reflecting on Past Experiences

While you're crafting a new identity, don't forget to reflect on your past. It's not about dwelling on it, but learning from it. Every experience, good or bad, is a brushstroke in the bigger picture of your life.

Learning From The Past

- **Understanding Your Journey:** Look at your past experiences through a lens of understanding and growth.
- **Forgiving and Moving Forward:** Practice forgiveness, both towards yourself and others, as a way to move forward without baggage.

Wrapping Up

As we conclude Chapter 18, remember, rediscovering yourself in sobriety is a journey of exploration, growth, and creativity. It's about embracing every part of you, crafting an identity that reflects your truest self, and stepping confidently into the world as the new, sober you.

CHAPTER 19: "STAYING STEADY: BUILDING RESILIENCE FOR LONG-TERM SOBRIETY"

Welcome to Chapter 19! As we journey further into the heartlands of recovery, it's time to talk about resilience – that superhero quality that keeps you going strong, no matter what life throws at you. Imagine resilience as your personal force field in the epic saga of sobriety. It's not about never falling; it's about always getting back up, dusting off, and marching forward with a wink and a smile.

The Pillars of Resilience

Building resilience is like constructing a fortress where your sobriety can thrive. It involves a mix of mental, emotional, and physical strategies.

Strengthening Your Mental Muscles

- **Positive Thinking:** Cultivate a mindset of optimism. It's not about wearing rose-colored glasses but choosing to see the silver lining in every cloud.
- **Problem-Solving Skills:** Develop the ability to tackle challenges head-on, turning obstacles into stepping stones.

Emotional Resilience: The Heart of the Matter

Your emotional resilience is key in navigating the highs and lows of recovery. It's about managing your emotions in a way that's healthy and constructive.

Techniques For Emotional Fortitude

- **Emotional Awareness:** Recognize and understand your emotions. It's like being an emotional detective, decoding the clues of your feelings.
- **Healthy Expression:** Find safe and healthy ways to express your emotions – through art, conversation, or physical activity.

Physical Resilience: Body as the Temple

Your physical health significantly impacts your ability to maintain sobriety. Your body body supports a resilient mind.

Nurturing Physical Health

- **Regular Exercise:** Engage in physical activities that you enjoy. It not only keeps you fit but also releases endorphins, boosting your mood and resilience.
- **Balanced Diet:** Eat nutritious foods that fuel your body and mind. Think of your diet as premium gas for your car – the better the fuel, the smoother the ride.
- **Adequate Rest:** Never underestimate the power of a good night's sleep. It's like hitting the reset button on your brain.

Social Resilience: The Strength of Connections

Resilience is also about drawing strength from those around you. Your relationships can be a powerful source of support and encouragement.

Fostering Supportive Relationships

- **Building a Support Network:** Surround yourself with people who uplift and support you. These relationships can be your safety net on tough days
- **Seeking Help When Needed:** Don't be afraid to reach out for help. Whether it's a counselor, a support group, or a trusted friend, asking for help is a sign of strength, not weakness.

Continuous Learning and Growth

Resilience is also about growth and adaptation. Embrace learning as a lifelong journey – every new skill or insight adds to your resilience arsenal.

Embracing New Challenges

- **Stay Curious:** Keep exploring new interests and hobbies. It's like adding new tools to your toolbox – you never know when they'll come in handy.
- **Learn from Setbacks:** View every challenge as a learning opportunity. It's not about how many times you fall, but how much you learn each time you get back up.

Wrapping Up

As we wrap up Chapter 19, remember that building resilience is a continuous process. It's about cultivating a strong mind, a healthy body, and a network of support. Your journey in sobriety is a testament to your strength and resilience. Keep building, keep growing, and keep moving forward, one step at a time.

CHAPTER 20: "HORIZONS UNBOUND: CHARTING A LIFELONG JOURNEY IN SOBRIETY"

Welcome to Chapter 20, the closing chapter of this section on the gateway to your endless journey in sobriety. Here, we stand at the cusp of a new era, not just as survivors of addiction but as architects of our own lives. Imagine yourself at the helm of a ship, sailing towards horizons unbound with the vast ocean of life ahead, ripe with possibilities, challenges, and adventures.

The Voyage of Lifelong Sobriety

This journey is not a sprint; it's a marathon, a continuous voyage that evolves and grows as you do. It requires endurance, adaptability, and a compass of self-awareness to navigate through calm and stormy weathers alike.

Crafting Your Sobriety Map

• Dynamic Strategies for Changing Tides: Sobriety, much like life, is ever static. Develop strategies that are flexible and can adapt to life's ever-changing scenarios.
• Continual Learning and Adaptation: Stay open to learning, whether it's from books, people, or your own experiences. Each lesson is a tool in your navigational kit.

Constructing a Fulfilling Life in Sobriety

CHAPTER 20: "HORIZONS UNBOUND: CHARTING A LIFELONG JOURNEY IN SOBRIETY"

Welcome to Chapter 20, the closing chapter of this section, yet the gateway to your endless journey in sobriety. Here, we stand at the cusp of a new era, not just as survivors of addiction but as architects of our own lives. Imagine yourself at the helm of a ship, sailing towards horizons unbound, with the vast ocean of life ahead, ripe with possibilities, challenges, and adventures.

The Voyage of Lifelong Sobriety

This journey is not a sprint; it's a marathon, a continuous voyage that evolves and grows as you do. It requires endurance, adaptability, and a compass of self-awareness to navigate through calm and stormy weathers alike.

Crafting Your Sobriety Map

- **Dynamic Strategies for Changing Tides:** Sobriety, much like life, is not static. Develop strategies that are flexible and can adapt to life's ever-changing scenarios.
- **Continual Learning and Adaptation:** Stay open to learning, whether it's from books, people, or your own experiences. Each lesson is a tool in your navigational kit.

Constructing a Fulfilling Life in Sobriety

Beyond the absence of addiction lies the canvas of your life, waiting for you to paint it with vibrant colors of joy, purpose, and fulfillment.

Building Blocks Of A Meaningful Life

- **Pursuing Passions:** Rediscover old passions or cultivate new ones. Let these activities not just fill your time but enrich your soul.
- **Goal Setting and Dream Chasing:** Set goals that challenge, excite, and motivate you. Break them into achievable steps and celebrate each milestone, no matter how small.

Transitioning to "War Stories"

As we segue into "War Stories," prepare yourself for a deep dive into the heart of addiction and recovery through the lens of others' experiences. These stories are raw, real, and resonant, offering a mosaic of the human experience in its fight against addiction.

Embracing The Power Of Storytelling

- **Learning from Diverse Journeys:** Every story in "War Stories" brings a unique perspective. Be open to the lessons they offer, even when they differ from your own experience.
- **Finding Connection in Shared Struggles:** These stories underscore the universal struggles and triumphs in recovery. They remind us that while our journeys are personal, we are not alone in them.
- **The Ripple Effect:** Influencing and InspiringYour journey of recovery, marked by its trials and triumphs, doesn't just reshape your life; it has the potential to touch and inspire others.

Your Role In The Recovery Tapestry

- **Sharing Your Narrative:** When you're ready, sharing your story can be a powerful act of healing for yourself and others. It's a way of giving back and strengthening the fabric of the recovery community.
- **Living as an Example:** Embody the principles of recovery in your everyday life. Your actions, attitude, and approach to challenges can serve as an inspiration to those around you.

Closing Reflections

As this chapter closes, reflect on the journey you've undertaken. From the shadows of addiction to the light of recovery, you have traversed a path many fear to tread. The road ahead is replete with opportunities for continuous growth, learning, and joy. Embrace it with the knowledge that your journey is both a personal triumph and a beacon of hope for others.

WAR STORIES: REAL-LIFE STORIES FROM THE FRONTLINE OF ADDICTION AND THEIR HARD-FOUGHT JOURNEY TO SOBRIETY

#1 *"The Empty Bottle"* - David's Story of Alcohol Addiction

The Descent

David had always been the life of the party, a successful lawyer who could charm a courtroom or light up a gathering. His evenings often ended with a glass of Scotch - a ritual that slowly morphed from a pleasure to a need. At first, it was just to unwind after long hours at the firm, but gradually, the quantity increased, and the reasons blurred.His wife, Jenna, began to express concern as evenings turned into nights with David increasingly distant, glass in hand. Arguments became frequent, revolving around his drinking and neglect of family time. David's response was denial and irritation. "It's just a drink. It helps me relax. You're overreacting," he'd retort.Work started to suffer too. Mornings were groggy, and his once sharp mind felt clouded. Deadlines were missed, and clients began to notice. Yet, the more his life seemed to unravel, the more he found refuge in the numbing embrace of alcohol.

The Wake-Up Call

The wake-up call came harshly and unexpectedly. One night, driving home from a bar, David was stopped by the police. The subsequent DUI charge was a jolt. The look of disappointment in Jenna's eyes was worse than any legal reprimand. David realized his 'harmless habit' was a full-blown addiction that was endangering not just his career and marriage, but lives.

The Road To Recovery

The DUI was a turning point. David, grappling with guilt and a dawning realization, decided to attend Alcoholics Anonymous

(AA) meetings. The first meeting was intimidating. He sat in the back, silently listening to stories that echoed his own. There was an odd comfort in knowing he wasn't alone.Jenna, although skeptical, supported his efforts. She saw the man she loved trying to emerge from the haze of alcohol. David started therapy, confronting not just his addiction, but the underlying stress and insecurities he had been numbing with alcohol.

New Beginnings

Months passed. The journey was anything but linear. There were days of immense struggle, where the lure of alcohol seemed overpowering. But David held on. The support from his AA group was invaluable. They were his anchor on days when everything else seemed adrift.Slowly, David began to rediscover parts of himself lost to addiction. He started enjoying simple pleasures - playing with his kids, weekend family outings, and evenings filled with genuine, sober laughter. Work improved too; his mind was clear, and his arguments in court were sharp and persuasive once again.

Reflections And Hope

A year into his recovery, David reflected on his journey. The scars of his addiction were still there - in strained relationships and hard memories - but so was healing. He had learned to forgive himself, to rebuild, and to live a life not dulled by alcohol, but enriched by sobriety's clarity.David knew the road ahead wouldn't always be easy, but he felt equipped to face it head-on, with honesty, support, and a renewed sense of purpose. His story was one of many in the tapestry of recovery, a testament to the resilience of the human spirit and the transformative power of sobriety.

#2 "Chasing Shadows" - Emily's Story of Heroin Addiction

The Descent Into Darkness

Emily's descent into heroin's clutches began subtly. A talented art student, her life was a canvas of potential. But pressures mounted – her perfectionism in art school, her strained relationship with her family, and the social circles that glamorized substance use. At first, heroin seemed like a temporary escape, a way to feel euphoria amidst the chaos of her life. It promised relief and delivered enslavement.Her days soon revolved around her next fix. The art, which was once her passion, became a distant memory. Relationships crumbled as Emily withdrew into the shadowy embrace of addiction. Heroin was a demanding master, and she became a mere shadow of her vibrant self.

Hitting Rock Bottom

Rock bottom came the night Emily overdosed in a dingy apartment, surrounded by strangers. Waking up in the hospital, she saw the worry and exhaustion etched on her parents' faces. The reality of her situation crashed down on her. She was teetering on the edge, her life a thread about to snap.

A Flicker Of Hope

It was her art professor who visited her in the hospital and offered a flicker of hope. He spoke of her talent and potential, of the beauty she could create in this world. His words pierced the fog of her addiction, igniting a tiny spark of desire for change.Rehabilitation was tough. Detox was a physical and mental battleground. But beyond the physical withdrawal, it was confronting her emotional pain that was the most challenging. Therapy sessions felt like peeling layers off a wound, but with each layer, she found more of herself.

Rediscovering Herself

Emily began to use art as a tool for her recovery. She poured her pain, guilt, and hope onto canvases. Each brushstroke was a conversation, a way of processing her journey from addiction to sobriety. Art became her therapy, her voice, and her identity.She also found strength in support groups, connecting with others who shared similar battles. Their stories and struggles, different yet so similar, gave her a sense of belonging and understanding she had long missed.

A New Dawn

Years into recovery, Emily held her first art exhibition – a collection that narrated her descent into addiction and her climb back to life. It was raw, powerful, and deeply personal. Her family was there, tears and pride in their eyes. Her professor, now more a mentor and friend, stood by her side.Emily knew the road ahead wouldn't be without its challenges, but she also knew she had the tools and support to face them. Her story was a testament to the resilience of the human spirit and the transformative power of recovery. She wasn't just chasing shadows anymore; she was chasing light.

#3 "Pill to Pain" - John's Story of Prescription Drug Addiction

An Unexpected Beginning

John's journey into addiction was one he never expected. A car accident left him with a painful back injury and a prescription for painkillers. Initially, they were a relief, a necessary aid in his recovery. But slowly, the pills became more than a remedy; they became a necessity.His life, once active and full, began to shrink around his next dose. The painkillers numbed more than his physical pain – they began to dull his emotions, his relationships, and his ambitions. Work became a struggle, as keeping up with the demands while managing his growing dependency was exhausting.

The Escalation

The dosage that once provided relief was no longer effective. John found himself taking more pills, more often. The realization that he might be addicted came with a mix of denial and fear. He tried to stop, only to be met with overwhelming withdrawal symptoms and unmanageable pain.His wife, Lisa, began to notice the empty pill bottles hidden away, the mood swings, and his increasing withdrawal from family life. Confrontations led to arguments, with John defensively insisting he had everything under control.

The Turning Point

The turning point came when Lisa found John unconscious, surrounded by pill bottles. The emergency room visit was a blur, but the doctor's words were crystal clear: "You're lucky to be alive. It's time to get help."Facing the truth of his addiction, John agreed to enter a rehabilitation program. The detox process was grueling, filled with both physical and emotional turmoil. Group therapy sessions felt invasive at first, but gradually, they became a source of comfort and understanding.

Rebuilding And Recovery

In rehab, John learned about the nature of addiction. He attended workshops that taught him alternative pain management techniques, like meditation and gentle exercise. He began to understand how his dependency developed and how to rebuild his life without relying on pills.Reconnecting with Lisa and his children was not easy. There was hurt and distrust that needed healing. But through family therapy and open communication, they began to mend the fractures in their relationships.

A New Chapter

Now, two years into sobriety, John volunteers at a local community center, sharing his story and helping others understand the risks of prescription drug addiction. He's back at work, enjoying his job and the challenges it brings.John knows the road to recovery is a lifelong journey. He has his support group, his family, and a set of tools to help him manage both his physical pain and the challenges of life. His story is a reminder that addiction can happen to anyone and that recovery, though difficult, is possible with help and commitment.

#4"Speed of Life" - Mark's Story of Methamphetamine Addiction

The Fast Lane

Mark's journey into the world of methamphetamine began at a party during his late twenties. He was instantly drawn to the drug's ability to make him feel euphoric, powerful, and seemingly unstoppable. Mark was working two jobs and struggling to keep up, and meth seemed like the solution to all his problems. It gave him the energy to work long hours, the confidence to socialize, and the escape from the pressures of everyday life.

Losing Control

But the escape soon became a prison. Mark's casual use spiraled into a daily necessity. His life revolved around his next high. He started neglecting his responsibilities, losing one job after another. Relationships with friends and family deteriorated as he became more erratic and isolated.The turning point came when Mark was arrested for possession. Sitting in a jail cell, he realized how far he had fallen. He barely recognized himself – the once ambitious, life-loving individual now just a shadow, consumed by addiction.

The Road To Recovery

After his release, Mark knew he needed to change. He entered a rehabilitation program, where the detox process was a brutal awakening. Withdrawal symptoms were intense, and facing the reality of his addiction was even harder.Therapy sessions were tough. Mark had to confront the underlying issues that led him to addiction – the insecurities, the fear of failure, and the inability to cope with stress. He learned about the psychological grip of methamphetamine and how it had rewired his brain.

Rebuilding And Finding Support

In rehab, Mark found support in others who were fighting their own battles with addiction. Group sessions provided a sense of community and understanding. He also reconnected with his family, who supported him through his recovery journey.Mark took up exercise as a way to cope with stress and rebuild his physical strength. Running became a new passion, giving him a sense of achievement and freedom he once sought in drugs.

A New Purpose

Two years sober, Mark is now an advocate for drug abuse awareness and recovery. He speaks at schools and community centers, sharing his story to educate others about the dangers of methamphetamine. He has also rekindled his love for photography, using it as a creative outlet to express his journey and view the world with new eyes.Mark's story is one of redemption and resilience. It shows the destructive power of addiction but also the incredible strength of the human spirit to overcome it. His journey serves as a beacon of hope for those still trapped in the cycle of drug abuse, proving that recovery is possible and life can be rebuilt.

#5 "Invisible Chains" - Clara's Story of Cocaine Addiction

The Illusion Of Control

Clara's descent into addiction began in the glamorous world of advertising. As a creative director, she thrived in an environment of relentless deadlines and high-stakes pitches. Cocaine first entered her life as a secret weapon to maintain her edge, to stay on top, to be always 'on.'

The Cost Of A High

What started as an occasional boost quickly spiraled into dependency. Cocaine was no longer a choice; it was a necessity. Her life, once a carefully curated picture of success, began to unravel. At work, her once brilliant ideas were overshadowed by missed deadlines and erratic behavior. At home, the warm glow of family life dimmed to a flicker as Clara became more withdrawn.

The Turning Point

The facade came crashing down the night Clara was rushed to the ER after a binge. Lying in the hospital bed, the severity of her situation hit her. She was living a double life, and the part she hid was now threatening to destroy everything she valued.

Embracing Recovery

Admitting she needed help was Clara's first step toward recovery. Detox was a harrowing experience, stripping her not just of the drug, but also of the persona she had built around it. In rehab, she confronted her addiction head-on, unraveling the layers of denial and self-deception. Group therapy became her haven, a place where she could be vulnerable and honest.

A New Chapter

Recovery brought Clara a clarity she hadn't realized she'd lost. She found new ways to channel her creativity and energy, rediscovering passions she had neglected. She began to use her experience to advocate for mental health and substance abuse awareness in the corporate world.Clara's journey is a testament to the deceptive nature of addiction and the courage required to break free from its grip. Her story, from the highs of addiction to the lows of recovery and back to a new, sober reality, is a powerful narrative of resilience and redemption.

#6 "Ecstasy's Edge" - Lucas's Story of MDMA/ Ecstasy Addiction

The Party Begins

Lucas's descent into ecstasy addiction started under strobe lights and thumping bass. As a college student, he was drawn to the rave scene for its promise of escapism and euphoria. Ecstasy, or MDMA, was the key to what felt like a higher state of being - more connected, more alive. Initially, it was just for the weekends, a way to let loose and break free from the pressures of his studies.

Blurring Reality

But the party soon spilled over into his everyday life. Lucas began using ecstasy more frequently, chasing the fleeting high and the profound sense of connection it offered. His academic performance suffered, and his relationships outside the party scene started to fray. The drug, once a gateway to paradise, became a crutch.

The Cost Of Ecstasy

The turning point for Lucas came after a night of heavy use led to a terrifying experience of hallucinations and paranoia. He was found by a friend, disoriented and scared, a shadow of his usual confident self. It was a jarring glimpse into the potential dangers of his lifestyle.

Confronting The Habit

Admitting he had a problem was Lucas's first step on a long road to recovery. Detoxing from ecstasy was physically and emotionally taxing. He struggled with feelings of depression and disconnection, the stark contrast to the artificial highs of the drug.Rehabilitation brought Lucas face to face with the realities he had been avoiding - his insecurities, his fear of failure, and his need for genuine connections.

Rediscovering Himself

Through therapy, support groups, and a renewed focus on his art, Lucas began to rebuild his life. He found new ways to experience joy and connection, rediscovering passions that ecstasy had overshadowed.Now several years sober, Lucas mentors young people about the risks of drug abuse. His story is a testament to the deceptive allure of ecstasy and the strength it takes to reclaim control. His journey from the highs of addiction to the reality of recovery is a powerful narrative of resilience and hope.

#7 "The Synthetic Trap" - Kevin's Story of Synthetic Drug Addiction

A Dangerous Curiosity

Kevin's journey into the world of synthetic drugs began with curiosity and a desire for something new. At college parties, he was introduced to synthetic substances, often marketed as safe and legal alternatives to traditional drugs. The initial experiences were exhilarating, offering Kevin a sense of adventure and escape.

A Deceptive Descent

However, the unpredictable nature of synthetic drugs quickly took a toll on Kevin. The effects became increasingly erratic, with intense highs followed by severe lows. His academic performance plummeted, and his relationships began to suffer. Kevin found himself in a cycle of using more to escape the growing problems in his life.

The Harsh Reality

The turning point came when Kevin experienced a severe adverse reaction, landing him in the emergency room. The terrifying experience was a stark wake-up call. He realized that the synthetic drugs, once a source of excitement, were now a threat to his life.

The Road To Recovery

Recovery for Kevin was a journey back from the edge. He entered a rehab program specialized in dealing with synthetic drug addiction. The process was challenging, as Kevin dealt with intense withdrawal symptoms and the psychological grip of addiction.In rehab, he learned about the dangerous unpredictability of synthetic substances and began to understand the underlying reasons for his drug use. Group therapy sessions provided him with support and a sense of community.

Building A New Life

Kevin's recovery was a gradual process of rebuilding his life and rediscovering who he was without the influence of drugs. He re-enrolled in college, this time focusing on his studies and rebuilding relationships he had neglected.Kevin now volunteers at local high schools, sharing his story to educate students about the dangers of synthetic drugs. His journey is a powerful reminder of the risks of these substances and the importance of making informed choices. His story of recovery and redemption offers hope and serves as a warning about the perils of synthetic drug experimentation.

#8 "Hidden in Plain Sight" - Rachel's Story of Inhalant Addiction

An Innocuous Beginning

Rachel's journey into inhalant addiction began with a curiosity that seemed harmless at first. As a high school student, she was introduced to inhalants at a party – everyday household products that were easily accessible and promised a quick high. It started as an occasional thrill, a way to fit in and escape the pressures of adolescence.

The Descent Into Dependency

But what started as occasional use soon spiraled into a dangerous habit. Rachel found herself using inhalants more frequently, chasing the fleeting euphoria they provided. Her schoolwork suffered, friendships faltered, and her once bright and outgoing personality dimmed. The very products that were commonplace in her home had become the chains of her addiction.

A Wake-Up Call

The wake-up call came harshly. Rachel was found unconscious by her younger brother, a can of aerosol still in her hand. The fear and confusion in her brother's eyes were a jolt of reality. She realized that her secret addiction was no longer just affecting her but also those she loved.

Confronting The Addiction

Addiction to inhalants was a difficult and harrowing battle for Rachel. Despite her efforts in rehabilitation, the damage inflicted by prolonged inhalant abuse had taken a severe toll on her health. The program provided her with a brief respite, a glimpse into a life free from the grip of addiction. However, the physical consequences of her inhalant use were severe and irreversible.

A Tragic End

Tragically, Rachel's story doesn't have the happy ending that many hope for in their journey to recovery. A few months after completing her rehabilitation program, Rachel suffered a fatal cardiac arrest, a direct result of the long-term effects of inhalant abuse on her heart.Her passing was a devastating blow to her family, friends, and the community that had supported her through her recovery. Rachel's story became a poignant reminder of the dangers of inhalant abuse, particularly its deceptive and often underestimated lethal potential.

Legacy And Lessons

In the wake of her death, Rachel's family worked to raise awareness about the dangers of inhalant addiction. They shared her story with schools and community groups, highlighting the risks associated with seemingly harmless household products.Her story serves as a powerful warning about the often-overlooked dangers of inhalant abuse. It underscores the importance of early intervention and the need for more awareness and education on the topic. Rachel's life and untimely death remind us that addiction can have many faces, and its consequences can be tragically irreversible.

The Beginnings Of A Spiral

Jordan's journey into the world of poly-substance addiction began in his late teens. What started with experimentation at parties soon turned into a tangled web of various substances. Alcohol, marijuana, prescription pills—each offered a different escape, a different way to cope with his insecurities and the pressures he felt from his environment.

The Deepening Maze

Each substance played a different role in Jordan's life. Alcohol was for socializing, pills for stress, marijuana for relaxation. But together, they created a complex maze of dependency that Jordan couldn't navigate his way out of. His life became a cycle of using, recovering, and then using again to escape the discomfort of the come-downs.

Losing Himself

Jordan's addiction started affecting every aspect of his life. His performance at his job declined, leading to his eventual dismissal. Relationships became strained and eventually fell apart as he retreated further into his addiction. He rarely recognized himself—once a vibrant, ambitious individual now lost to a haze of substances.

The Moment Of Realization

The turning point came one evening when Jordan found himself alone in his apartment, surrounded by an array of substances.

91

#9 "The Tangled Web" - Jordan's Story of Poly-Substance Addiction

The Beginnings Of A Spiral

Jordan's journey into the world of poly-substance addiction began in his late teens. What started with experimentation at parties soon turned into a tangled web of various substances. Alcohol, marijuana, prescription pills – each offered a different escape, a different way to cope with his insecurities and the pressures he felt from his environment.

The Deepening Maze

Each substance played a different role in Jordan's life. Alcohol was for socializing, pills for stress, marijuana for relaxation. But together, they created a complex maze of dependency that Jordan couldn't navigate his way out of. His life became a cycle of using, recovering, and then using again to escape the discomfort of the come-downs.

Losing Himself

Jordan's addiction started affecting every aspect of his life. His performance at his job declined, leading to his eventual dismissal. Relationships became strained and eventually fell apart as he retreated further into his addiction. He barely recognized himself – once a vibrant, ambitious individual, now lost in a haze of substances.

The Moment Of Realization

The turning point came one evening when Jordan found himself alone in his apartment, surrounded by an array of substances, feeling emptier than ever. It was a moment of painful clarity – he realized he was trapped in a cycle that was slowly consuming him. He reached out to a friend, confessing the extent of his addiction for the first time.

The Road To Recovery

With support from his friend, Jordan sought help. Detoxing from multiple substances was an intense and daunting process. He faced not only physical withdrawal but also had to confront the emotional and mental issues that he had been numbing for so long. In rehab, Jordan attended various therapy sessions, including group therapy, where he connected with others who shared similar struggles. These connections were crucial in helping him understand he wasn't alone in his battle.

A New Path

Post-rehab, Jordan dedicated himself to recovery. He joined support groups, continued therapy, and took up hobbies that he had abandoned. He found solace in music and art, rediscovering parts of himself that had been lost in addiction.

Giving Back

Years into his recovery, Jordan now works as a counselor, helping others navigate the complexities of poly-substance addiction. He shares his story openly, hoping to shed light on the realities of this form of addiction and to offer hope to those still struggling. Jordan's story is a poignant example of how easily one can fall into the trap of poly-substance addiction and the strength and perseverance it takes to claw out of it. His journey serves as a reminder of the power of human resilience and the importance of seeking and offering support in the face of addiction.

#10 "A Rebel's Road" - My Story of Addiction And Start on The Road to Recovery

The Descent Begins

Between the ages of 30 and 32, my life teetered on the edge. I overdosed four times, each incident a glaring sign of my deepening addiction. Despite these close encounters with death, my use of fentanyl continued unabated, supplemented by meth to keep myself awake, to keep my heart rate and breathing from bottoming out. It was a dangerous game, one that I played recklessly, without regard for the consequences.

Love, Loss, And Rock-Bottom

At 34, in the midst of this turmoil, I met Chelsey, the girl of my dreams. She was entangled in her own battle with meth, but fentanyl was not yet part of her story, not until she began using it with me. Introducing her to fentanyl is a decision that haunts me, a regret that weighs heavily on my soul. Together, we spiraled further down the rabbit hole of addiction, losing sight of everything else. The addiction cost me dearly: my children, my home, and my job. Yet, none of these losses were enough to jolt me into seeking sobriety. I resorted to hustling, to committing crimes, just to keep feeding the addiction.

The Spiral Continues

Then, in October 2023, tragedy struck. I lost Chelsey to this relentless disease called addiction. Her death sent me into an even deeper spiral. My usage skyrocketed to 50 pills or more a day, and when that wasn't enough to numb the emotional, mental, and physical pain, I turned to using pure fentanyl powder. I wasn't even getting high anymore, just trying to maintain and stave off sickness. I knew deep down I was actively trying to join Chelsey, as I didn't have the tools to cope with the loss.

My mother, witnessing my decline, called or texted me every day, just to make sure I was still alive. It's heartbreaking to realize the agony I put her through. This was how low I had sunk, causing unimaginable pain and worry to the woman who gave me life.

A Pivotal Dream

The turning point came unexpectedly. The night before Christmas Eve, I had a dream about Chelsey. She came to me, saying, "You promised me you would go to rehab." That morning, I told my mom, "I need to go to Rehab." Her reaction was a mix of tears and relief, as she said, "This is the first time you have ever asked me to go to rehab.

Choosing Life

The day after Christmas, December 26th, which is also the eldest of my younger sister's sobriety date, marking three years sober for her, became my sobriety date. We saw it as a beautiful thing to share. However, like many addicts about to enter rehab, I sought one last high. I went and did every drug I could get my hands on – fentanyl, meth, cocaine, marijuana, even crack. This was a dangerous path, but I felt it was necessary, a common yet perilous mindset among those about to embark on the road to recovery.

The Road To Recovery

Detox wasn't as bad as I anticipated, thanks to a buprenorphine taper, gabapentin, and other medications, including one to help me sleep. This medical support made the process more bearable than I had expected. In detox and rehab, I found a sense of camaraderie with my fellow recovering addicts.

We shared stories and experiences, learning from each other. The smoking area became a place of bonding and profound conversations, a stark contrast to the isolation I had experienced in my addiction.

Building A New Life

I'm now emerging from the fog of my addiction. My journey to sobriety is a testament to the power of resilience and the human spirit's capacity for change. I've learned to navigate the challenges of life with the tools I've acquired in recovery. I went to sober living and continue to build my sober support system. Sober living after treatment gives the opportunity to make friends and commrades-in-arms thru sobriety. Non-addicts dont usually understand what we have gone thru or why we "just can't stop doing drugs or drinking." Sober living gives you that community that everyone is in the same shoes. Now, my sober days are multiplying, and the good days are beginning to outnumber the bad. Most days I walk this sober road are filled with sunshine, yet there are still rainy days, of course. However, now I have the gear and tools to weather any storm that comes my way.

A Message Of Hope

For anyone reading this and struggling with addiction, know that you are not alone. Recovery is daunting, but it's possible. Explore different sobriety communities, find what resonates with you, and build your own recovery road. The journey is challenging, but remember, you are loved, and you are worthy of a better life.

AFTERWORD

As we come to the close of "A Rebel's Road: A Rebel's Guide to Recovery," I hope you've found within these pages not just a guide, but a companion on your journey to sobriety. Writing this book has been an exploration of my own path, a reflection on the twists and turns that have led me to where I stand today—firmly in the belief that recovery is as individual as the person undertaking it.

If there's one thing I wish for you to take away from this book, it's the understanding that your recovery journey is uniquely yours. It may not fit into the conventional frameworks we so often hear about, and that's perfectly okay. Sobriety doesn't have to look a certain way; it just has to work for you.

Throughout "A Rebel's Road," I've shared laughs, lessons, and a few of the scars I've picked up along the way. But more than anything, I've shared the unshakeable belief that recovery is possible for everyone. No matter how many times you've stumbled or how lost you may feel, there is always a path that leads to brighter days.

As you move forward, remember to carry with you the spirit of rebellion that challenges you to find your own way, the courage to face the unknown, and the wisdom to know that you don't have to walk this road alone. The community of rebels, misfits, and dreamers is vast, and there is strength in our shared experiences.

Thank you for allowing me to be a part of your journey. May "A Rebel's Road" be a reminder that in the face of addiction, there's always hope, always a choice, and always a chance to redefine what recovery means to you.

Here's to the road ahead, to the laughter, the tears, and everything in between. Keep forging your path, keep believing in your strength, and never forget that being a rebel can be your greatest asset in recovery.

With gratitude and solidarity,

-Zachary

ABOUT THE AUTHOR

Zachary B. Gorman

In the heart of a rebel beats the story of resilience, recovery, and the rediscovery of life beyond addiction. The author of "A Rebel's Road: A Rebel's Guide to Recovery" is not just a writer but a warrior who has navigated the tumultuous waters of addiction to find sobriety on their own terms.

With a life once overshadowed by the struggles of substance abuse, the author embarked on a journey that many find daunting. Yet, through the trials and tribulations, a unique path to recovery was carved, one that defied conventional methods and expectations. This journey, marked by moments of despair, enlightenment, and eventual triumph, forms the backbone of their narrative.

A self-proclaimed maverick, the author brings to the table an unfiltered, humorous, and profoundly honest account of their road to recovery. Their writing is a reflection of their belief that sobriety doesn't have to be a solemn affair but can be a journey of self-discovery, laughter, and unexpected joy.

Beyond the pages, the author is an advocate for finding one's own route to recovery, encouraging others to embrace their individuality in their sobriety journey. With "A Rebel's Road," they hope to inspire those who feel out of place in traditional recovery settings, offering a beacon of hope and a reminder that recovery, much like life, is a personal adventure.

In their free time, the author enjoys exploring the great outdoors,spending time with family & friends, engaging in spontaneous adventures, and sharing stories that unite the spirits of fellow rebels walking the road to recovery.

Made in United States
Troutdale, OR
12/05/2024

25939349R00066